Sparkling Gems From Within
Presents

A Light Energy that sparkles inside of YOU!

Did you know that you can bring more happiness into your life by simply choosing to be happy?

PARENTS:
Have fun with your children as you explore a simple and easy way to recognize the gift of happiness you already hold inside.

· ·

The enclosed CD contains:

A narration with songs and poems that compliment our little *"Hi—I'm Happy!"* Book. The songs, listed below, are written and sung by the author— and are very much a part of our journey into happiness.

1) LOOK TO THE CHILDREN
2) HAPPY, I AM!
3) I AM A BEAUTIFUL CHILD OF GOD
4) THINKING RIGHT
5) LOOK TO THE GOOD

The poem is titled I'M VERY HAPPY TO BE ME.

There are 2 more books and CDs in this series.

Book 2: "Hi-I'm Love"   Book 3: "Sh-h-ish, I'm Peace"
These books will be available soon.

Hi—I'm Happy!

Copyright number TXul-130-738

All rights reserved. No part of this book or CD may be reproduced, stored in a retrieval system or transmitted in any form or by any means—electronic, mechanical, digital, photocopy, recording or any other means—except for brief quotations in printed reviews, without the prior permission of the author.
Printer info and number info here.

ISBN: 0-88144234-8

Dedicated to all the children of the world: Ages 3 to 103

Acknowledgements

There are many precious people who have touched my life with their 'light' of love. This blessing helped me to bring these little sparkling gems, from within, to life.

Thanks to Larry Wayne and Grace Johnston who gave me the gift of Truth, which lead me to the realization that I am special too!

Thanks to my family for their love and encouragement. My beautiful grandchildren have been a great source of inspiration to me.

Thanks to Annie, your sparkle came forth from within and painted itself in all of the pictures you created.

My thanks and appreciation to Mark for his instrumental music played from the heart, and to Carol for her unique skills in photography.

Introduction for Parents

It is so wonderful to teach our children the names of the colors, the numbers and the letters of the alphabet. We are proud when we hear them recite these teachings. Much praise is given to our little ones for 'doing' these things.

Let us also give praise and encouragement for what our children are 'BEING.'

For example, we might say, "Oh, you are BEING HAPPY, kind, responsible, loving; good for you!"

By saying this we will help our children remember who they really are. They can be encouraged to recognized the 'SPARKLING GEMS' that shine within each and every one of us.

HAPPY! Is our first 'Little Sparkling Gem' From Within. Remember him and welcome him into your heart!

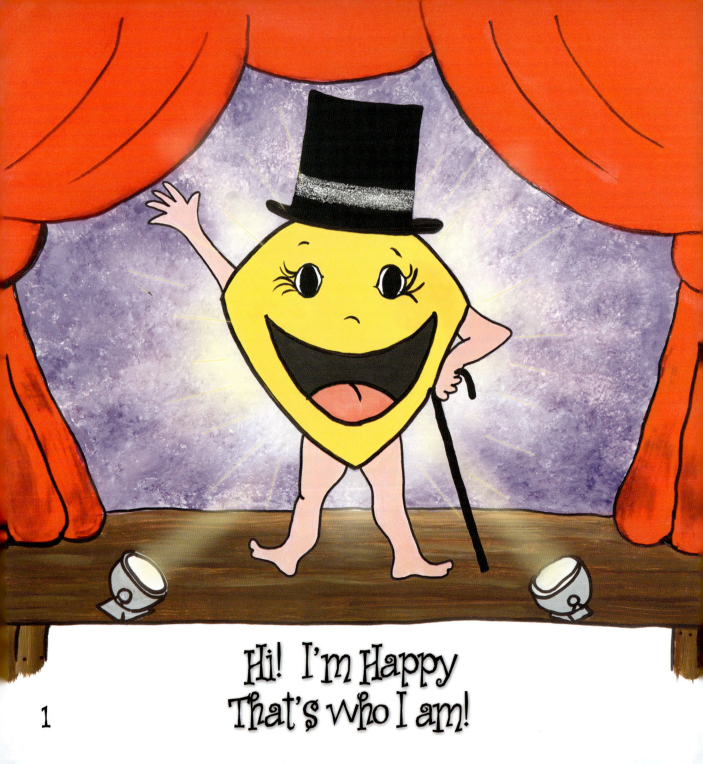
Hi! I'm Happy That's who I am!

I'm not Jelly and
I'm not Jam

I'm a Sparkling Gem
That you can see

Do you know where I can be found?

I'm tucked inside you
Safe and sound

You keep me sparkling
When you laugh, sing and play

But when you are sad
Or when you are angry

Dark clouds hide my sparkle
So you can't find me

Please ask me out again
To sparkle and play

To make the clouds disappear
So I can be seen

Just use your magic words
And you will know where I've been

And POOF! I'm sparkling
In rain or in sun

Now we can go on
And have lots of fun

At night just before
You drift off to sleep

Remember that 'Happy'
Is inside you deep!

A Gift From HAPPY For The Whole Family

I'm Very Happy To Be Me
-By Shirley Anne Burroughs-

I'm very happy to be me
There's no one else I'd rather be.
God created me for goodness sakes
And He doesn't make mistakes.

I may not find my way to fame,
Nor with vast fortune stake my claim,
But the happiness within my heart
Makes me certain how to play my part.

I'll add goodness each and every day,
As I endeavor not to take away,
For nothing greater can be done
Than to create love, peace and a little fun.

I know my happiness depends on me
And when I take charge, I will be free.
I'll seek the truth in word and deed,
I'll listen for the answers that I need.

Then each morning when I arise
And give thanks for the trees and skies,
I'll lift my head up, that I might see
And make certain to give thanks for me.

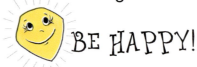 BE HAPPY!